Character Education

Caring

by Lucia Raatma

Consultant:
Madonna Murphy, Ph.D.
Associate Professor of Education
University of St. Francis, Joliet, Illinois
Author, *Character Education in America's
Blue Ribbon Schools*

Bridgestone Books
an imprint of Capstone Press
Mankato, Minnesota

Bridgestone Books are published by Capstone Press
151 Good Counsel Drive, P.O. Box 669, Mankato, Minnesota 56002
http://www.capstone-press.com

Library of Congress Cataloging-in-Publication Data
Raatma, Lucia.
    Caring/by Lucia Raatma.
    p. cm.—(Character education)
    Includes bibliographical references and index.
    Summary: Describes caring as a virtue and suggests ways in which caring
can be shown, such as recycling, donating to charity, helping others, and
listening.
    ISBN 0-7368-0366-1
    1. Caring—Juvenile literature. [1. Caring.] I. Title. II. Series.
BJ1475.R33   2000
177'.7—dc21

                                                                99-31306
                                                                CIP

Editorial Credits

Christy Steele, editor; Heather Kindseth, cover designer and illustrator;
    Kimberly Danger, photo researcher

Photo Credits

Archive/Popperfoto, 18
David F. Clobes, 8, 12
Shaffer Photography/James L. Shaffer, cover, 4
Unicorn Stock Photos/Martha McBride, 10; Dennis
    MacDonald, 14; Tom McCarthy, 16; Karen Holsinger Mullen, 20
Uniphoto, 6

2 3 4 5 6 06 05 04 03 02 01

Table of Contents

Caring

Caring means thinking about the needs of others. Caring people are kind. They try to help others. You can show you care in many ways. You can ask people how they are doing. You can listen to your friends. People value others who care about them.

Caring about Your Family

You can show your family that you care about them. You can be helpful and kind. You can read to your younger brother or sister. You can help your brother make his bed. You can hug your mother or father.

Caring about Your Classmates

You can be a caring person at school. Be kind to your classmates. Help them if they have problems. You can explain a math question to a classmate. You can show a new student around the library. You can listen to a classmate who is upset.

Caring about Yourself

Caring about yourself is important. You can do things you enjoy. Having fun will make you happy. You can take care of your body. Eat healthy foods and exercise. Get enough sleep each night. Brush your teeth every day. These actions will help you stay healthy.

Caring about Your Friends

Good friends show they care. You can show you care by listening to your friends. You can say something kind to your friends. Spending time with friends also shows you care. Maybe your friends need help learning a new game. You can show them how to play.

Caring about Others

Caring people often give their time and talents to help others. Sometimes you may have to put others' needs before your own. You may give your allowance to a friend to buy lunch. Your favorite show may be on TV. You could help your mother cook instead.

allowance

money given to someone regularly; parents may give children allowances for doing small jobs at home.

Caring about Your Community

You can care for your community in many ways. You can help people you do not know. You can give your old clothes and toys to charity. You also can care for the environment. Do not litter. Recycle cans, bottles, and newspapers instead of throwing them away.

charity
a group that raises money or collects goods to help people in need

"Let us keep the joy of loving in our hearts and share this joy with all we meet."
—From a letter by Mother Teresa

Caring and Mother Teresa

Mother Teresa was a nun who lived in India. She spent her life caring for others. She cared for sick and dying people. Mother Teresa set up places to care for children who do not have parents. She gave food to hungry people. Mother Teresa saved many lives.

Caring and You

Putting people's needs before your own sometimes is hard. But caring for others often will make others care about you. People value and respect caring people. Caring also will help you feel good about yourself. Caring may help change someone's life.

▼ Hands On: Start a Recycling Program

Recycling helps save the environment. Recycling makes used items into new products. Start a recycling program to show that you care about the environment.

What You Need
Four large paper bags
Markers

What You Do
1. Use the markers to label the bags. Write the word "cans" on one bag. Write "plastic" on another bag. Write "newspaper" on another bag. Write "cardboard" on the last bag.
2. Wash any used cans and plastic containers.
3. Sort your used items into the four bags. Put cans in the "cans" bag. Put plastic items such as milk containers in the "plastic" bag. Put old newspapers in the "newspaper" bag. Put cardboard in the "cardboard" bag.
4. Ask an adult to take you to a recycling center when the bags are full.
5. Label new bags and repeat the steps.

You can start a recycling program at home and at school. Ask your family and friends to care for the environment by recycling.

▼Words to Know

allowance (uh-LOU-uhnss)—money given to someone regularly; children may receive allowances for doing small jobs at home.

charity (CHA-ruh-tee)—a group that raises money or collects goods to help people in need

environment (en-VYE-ruhn-muhnt)—the natural world of the land, water, and air

litter (LIT-ur)—to throw garbage on the ground

recycle (ree-SYE-kuhl)—to make used items into new products; people can recycle items such as glass, plastic, newspapers, and aluminum cans.

▼ Read More

Canning, Shelagh. *Caring.* Doing the Right Thing. Vero Beach, Fla.: Rourke, 1999.

Clarke, Brenda. *Caring for Others.* Tales of Courage. Austin, Texas: Steck-Vaughn, 1990.

Moncure, Jane Belk. *The Child's World of Caring.* Plymouth, Minn.: Child's World, 1997.

▼ Internet Sites

Absolutely Whootie: Stories to Grow By
http://www.storiestogrowby.com
Adventures from the Book of Virtues Home Page
http://www.pbs.org/adventures
Earthforce
http://www.earthforce.org

▼ Index